From Team Mediocrity To Team Greatness

Marako Marcus

Published by Marako Marcus, 2021.

Copyright

While every precaution has been taken in the preparation of this book, the publisher assumes no responsibility for errors or omissions, or for damages resulting from the use of the information contained herein.

Prologue

E ver find yourself in a team that lacks collaboration?
Do you lead a team that needs the spark to improve?
This handbook aims to transform your team to greatness!

TEAMWORK, COMMUNICATION, inspiration... what do all these have in common? They are the key elements of a successful team. It makes a whole of difference between mediocrity and greatness.

I am going to start off this book with a little encounter I had. I conduct numerous team training programs for corporate clients. As part of my training, I design a challenge whereby teams use masking tape and balloons to build the tallest and most stable structure in a given period of time. To date, one team stands out most in teamwork. This particular team holds the record for the tallest, most beautiful, and stable balloon tower.

Typical teams will start off the challenge by charging into the fray, then fire-fight later. This team, however, started by having a focused discussion. They planned, brainstormed and came up with several designs. Then they took a quick vote. The self-appointed leader asked for consensus and any better suggestions. Everyone agreed to execute Plan A.

They divided themselves into three groups. Each group was tasked with a portion of the structure. Once they had each completed their section, they hoisted it up and connected the top way above their heads. The structure was a pyramid with a square base.

The team? A group of school students aged between 11 and 12. The most amazing thing is that they not only completed the challenge as the fastest team, they even sat in a circle around their masterpiece to "protect" it! In fact this team of kids did way better than any adult teams I have seen! Teamwork? Definitely so!

It was this experience that started me on a journey of exploring what it takes for teamwork to inspire a group of ordinary people, a mediocre team, to aspire great dreams and accomplish great things. This book is all about bringing teams from mediocrity to greatness!

CHANGE YOUR THOUGHTS and you change your world. - *Norman Vincent Peale*

Chapter One: Great Teams have Vision

The Story
   The monthly meeting of the employees of SecondBest Marketing begins with the boss Mr. ShortSight giving his usual address.

"Ladies and gentlemen, as usual, it has been an average year. Till date, we have yet to reach our mid-year sales target. We will be conducting routine rounds to check on each person's sales figures. Remember, When we fight fire well, we will survive. Let's keep our focus. Next month we will review the numbers once more. Each department is to keep your cost in check. Keep your fingers crossed. May we survive another month."

The well-repeated speech stirred the employees to yet another mundane month of bean counting and cost cutting. The top sales person, Miss Farsight, shook her head in disappointment: it was yet another month of looking at figures. "Where does our vision fit in, I wonder?"

She took a slow walk out of the meeting room, ironically walking under a large board with the words "Our Corporate Vision: Dream Far, Dream Big!"

MEDIOCRITY VERSUS GREATNESS
   Great Teams have Great Vision
   It seems so obvious that we need vision. In fact, almost every organization has their own set of values and corporate vision. Sometimes it is called Shared Vision. Ironically, this Shared Vision is not always shared, or is shared only by a certain group of people. Even possibly those at the top management.

I remember a training session I ran with an MNC. We were sharing how important it was to aim high. A manager mentioned aloud that it was fine to make mistakes or not complete a task in time as our clients could see our effort put in and would still believe in us the next time. I think we have to be very careful with statements like that. Although it may be true that clients can forgive our inadequacies, there is every chance that they will approach a competitor.

If we do not have a vision and aim high, then our competitors will. It is imperative to our survival how well the company will thrive to have a vision!

It is interesting to also note that every top team in the world has a vision. More importantly, employees believe in that vision. The top team could be a corporate company, it could even be a sports team, or even a famous university. Whatever it may be, a vision is important.

Sharing of a vision is also of critical importance. I don't mean simply a once-a-year affair where the management announces and possibly repeats the organization's vision. It is essential that the vision is regularly reinforced and cascaded into workable and understandable terms to every employee on the ground. It must mean something to each individual. If the vision has no meaning to most people, then it is time to communicate it down the line. At the management level, this vision must be clearly articulated.

In a small working team, sharing the vision is just as applicable. The relevance of a corporate vision may not be immediately clear when one is tackling small projects. What is needed, however, is for the team leader to articulate the team's vision, cascaded from the corporate vision. It can be simple, it can be interesting, it can be fun, but it must be articulated. That is a sign of a Great Team-to-be. After the project is over, review what went well and what could be improved. In the next upcoming project, aim a little higher and improve how we plan, deliver and achieve the objectives of the project.

One team I trained had some problems in achieving their goals. This showed up in the experiential activity that they took part during our training program. The reason was simple, no one knew what the Big Picture was, what the Vision was. After a short debrief, they repeated the activity. One person took up the challenge of being the leader and voiced out the vision. Soon, the team completed the activity in record time. Upon review, the team realized that back at work, they needed to always pen down or voice out their vision every time they are tasked with a project.

One small company I gave consultancy to had a great vision. It wanted to be the leading company in its field in the world! Sounds really ridiculous? Well, the Managing Director believed in it and he shared it constantly with his people. After going through two years of difficulties, this four-year-old company has four offices worldwide, and it is still growing. A Great Vision may sound crazy and farfetched to most. But it does not matter what others think. Once the employees believe in it, great things happen. Great Teams emerge!

I trained the management team of an organization as the first run of a teamworking series. During one of the activities, they came up with their practical interpretation of their corporate vision in relation to their business goals and direction. After the activity, each group shared what the vision meant to them. These were decorated and written beautifully on large flipcharts.

However, from our post-program reports, I realized that there was still a lack of communication of the vision to the rest of the staff. In order to create the same sense of direction, I proposed that the flipcharts be laminated, the photos enlarged and placed on a prominent wall which every staff member would be able to see. This was done after the program.

All staff could see what their own management team went through. When the other staff members came for the following runs, everyone was looking forward to the training as a result of that!

To enhance Team Vision, leaders may consider inviting each work team to develop their own set of vision that is aligned with those of the company's. It should reflect the characteristics of each team. Once a shared vision is agreed upon, each team can develop the "how-to" elements that resonate with the vision. These "how" statements should be made visible to everyone. I suggest creating a banner to put it near a team wall, or a website. This vision should be applied daily. This is certainly not a time-wasting activity. In fact, the time spent getting team members aligned will greatly reduce the number of fire-fighting or resulting problems later.

Everyone believes in a vision that is well communicated. Everyone believes in a vision when the leaders believe it. Everyone believes in a vision when everyone understands it. A company can be visionary when they have people believing together in the vision.

The most pathetic person in the world is someone who has sight, but has no vision. - Helen Keller

TAKEAWAYS

- Establish Team Vision by setting goals and evaluate team performance. Be sure to talk with members about the progress they are making toward established goals so that employees get a sense both of their success and of the challenges that lie ahead
- What do we really care about in performing our job?
- What does the word success mean to this team?
- What actions can we take to live up to our stated values?

Chapter Two: Great Teams Learn and Re-Learn

T he Story
Neville Nou-it-All is a Sales Manager of Learning R Us Corporation. He is tasked to start a project team to look into expanding business beyond the borders. He gets his team together quickly. The team argues over which strategy to approach the problem. They finally settle on the same approach that they had used for the last eight years.

Lindy Lik-to-Lern tells the team in the room that the strategy that they have selected had been tried many times with no success. She proposed doing a market research to find out why the approach failed, learn from it, and then source for new opportunities.

Neville Nou-it-All dismissed Lindy Lik-to-Lern's suggestion. "We've been doing fine for the last eight years, why reinvent the wheel?"

As usual, Learning R Us Corporation embarked on the same plan as before. Nothing new, nothing to change. Some people pointed out that the business results did not change either...

Interestingly, the motto of Learning R Us goes like this: "We Breathe to Learn"

MEDIOCRITY VERSUS GREATNESS

Great Teams Learn and Re-Learn

Basically, all teams go through five stages of learning. Not only do teams learn when they progresses through each of the stages, there are opportunities to re-learn as well. This basic model for team learning, I have coined using these five terminologies:

Scan, Trigger, Investigate, Negotiate, Observe

The first stage is to Scan. When teams are tasked with a challenge, they need to scan the problem to find out what exactly the challenge is. Teams can ask themselves the "Why?" question. This will help to narrow and clarify the problem faced.

Teams need to scan a problem for opportunities in order to come up with even better solutions. Never look at a problem via a problem-solving mode. Be open to ideas that may not initially solve the problem, but could actually add value to possible solutions.

Once a team has scanned the horizon to find out exactly what the problem is, the teams then continue to the next phase, the Trigger stage.

For the Trigger stage to go well, teams should have a culture where everyone wants to contribute ideas. As mentioned in my other book, "Yes! But...", we tend to say "yes, but" to ideas around us. We tend to put negativity into every possibility and tear down ideas. We tend to be critics rather than be constructors of new ideas. But once a culture of openness is in place, team members can execute the Trigger stage with confidence. At this stage, all ideas and possibilities are listed down. Every idea should be considered as an option – no matter how insane it may sound. It is from wild ideas that breakthrough solutions come about.

In fact, if we were to look at the process of brainstorming, the ideas that normally result within the first fifteen minutes are what we call "normal" ideas. They are typical ideas which don't require too much thinking. They normally fall into the category of "tried before" ideas. This is a good start. Allow the Trigger stage to go on longer, then the ideas will begin to flow. Make use of team brainstorming tools. Set yourselves a quota on ideas. Soon the ideas will flow like a river.

Remember, all ideas, including wild ones, should be written down as they will be filtered down to the workable ones at the next stage.

The third stage is the Investigate stage. At this stage, ideas are filtered via evaluation criteria created by the team. Typically, ideas are measured by two main factors: the likelihood of success and the effort or cost required to implement them. But don't just stop there, choose about three other ideas that are "interesting". These are ideas that seem to have value, but may not be cost effective.

The challenge is then to take these "interesting" ideas and see how they can be modified to work. Once the ideas have been narrowed down, we will then enter into the fourth stage of action planning.

This stage, also called the Negotiate stage, happens when teams discuss and write out an action plan to execute and implement the ideas they have selected as their solution. This stage is critical as numerous teams could come up with plenty of ideas, but do not actually do anything with them. This no action talk only syndrome will soon cause team members will lose heart as they no longer see the value of coming up with ideas. Things to note at this stage is to figure out what needs to be done, by whom and by when.

Finally, we reach the stage called Observe. This is when we look at the team decision and implementation to see what can be improved. This could take place as soon as a week after the implementation. It should be repeated over time, at the interval of, say every three to six months. As a result of this on-going review, teams will always progress in their learning and re-learning.

I remember a particular session which I ran for a team from Korea. They were tasked to buy raw materials and create a device that would enable a ping pong ball to move continuously for as long as possible. During the Trigger stage, I noticed that they were excited over a particular idea or concept.

Their initial idea came from a rocking chair. Soon, they came up with a way to make it work with the least amount of materials, thus lowering their cost. All they used was a marble, a ping pong ball and some masking tape! They cut open the top of the ping pong ball, stuck a marble to the base of the inside of the ping pong ball and pasted back the top. The ping pong ball could then rock back and forth for a lengthy period of time, and cost only a fraction of the amount which the other teams used. Their key strength was in developing the Trigger stage by not dismissing any ridiculous ideas. Instead, they built on the ideas and worked out a way to make the radical ideas work.

Another example of team learning was for a company I conducted training for. The training was held recently in Thailand. The team was split into their four respective country teams to simulate the real working environment.

They were then separated physically and could only communicate by shouting to each other. The entire team had to complete a combined task. What they did not know was that we had allocated resources differently across the different country teams. This was also to simulate the real world context where each country had a different amount of resources.

When the experiential activity started, discussions were made within each individual country team. However, the four individual teams did not actually communicate with each other. Each "team" came up with their own plan, but there was no consensus. Everyone did their own thing! In the end, they failed.

The activity was stopped and the team was given ten minutes to discuss about what they have learnt in round one, make adjustments and repeat the activity. They went through stage five – Observe. They realized that teams were not Scanning for the opportunities around them, they did not Trigger ideas as a team. Certainly, the Negotiate stage was poor as nothing was being implemented.

The activity was then repeated with great excitement and they achieved the goal in the second round!

Sometimes we need to Observe to see what can or needs to be improved. Great teams always learn and re-learn!

Learning is not compulsory... neither is survival. - W. Edwards Deming

TAKEAWAYS

- Encourage listening and brainstorming. For both leaders and team members alike, the first priority in creating consensus is to stimulate debate. Remember that team members are often afraid to disagree with one another and that this fear can lead your team to make mediocre decisions
- Encourage debate and you will then inspire creativity. That's how you'll spur your team on towards better results
- Be open to new ideas. Try not to use words like "from my experience..."
- Don't tear down ideas, it's really easy to be "critics" but difficult to be constructive. It takes effort. Learn to build on people's ideas. Use constructive lines like "That's a good idea..." or "How else do you think we can solve..."
- Establish the parameters of consensus-building sessions. Be sensitive to the frustration that can mount when the team is not achieving consensus. At the outset of your meeting, establish time limits, and work with the team to achieve consensus within those parameters
- Do not be too quick to reach a consensus. If an agreement is struck too quickly, be careful to probe individual team members to discover their real feelings about the proposed solution

Chapter Three: Great Teams have Trust

The Story
    In *TrustMore Law Corporation*, Danny DisTrust was in charge of Local Sales.

He had a lot of work to do and needed some help. He requested his Department Head to provide him with some assistance. Alison LittleTrouble, who was in charge of Overseas Sales was assigned to help him.

When Danny DisTrust heard that help was going to come from Alison LittleTrouble, he told the Department Head that he would rather work alone. When queried, Danny DisTrust told him about what he had heard from colleagues of another department. Apparently, Alison LittleTrouble tried to steal some clients from him. They had overheard a tele-conversation that Alison LittleTrouble had with a prospective local client. She told him that she could handle the sales enquiry when local sales was supposed to be handled by Danny DisTrust. He had no faith in working with someone like her.

The Department Head decided to find out more from the colleagues that had told Danny DisTrust what they had overheard. They all felt that the two should not work together as Alison LittleTrouble was not to be trusted

Finally, the Department Head called in Alison LittleTrouble. Then the truth was revealed. She had indeed answered a call from a local client, but the client was actually enquiring on behalf of their overseas branch!

By the time the Department Head informed Danny DisTrust that it was just a misunderstanding, Alison LittleTrouble decided that she could not work in an environment that was filled with distrust.

Alison LittleTrouble tendered in her resignation and returned the company's staff handbook to the office. Briefly, she glanced on the cover of the company's handbook for the last time. TrustMore's four corporate values are written across the front of the book. It read: "Trust, Relationships, Openness and Support"

MEDIOCRITY VERSUS GREATNESS
Great Teams have Trust

Sounds a little farfetched? Actually, the above story is a summarized version of some of the experiences I encountered in the course of my consulting work with companies. As part of our organization-wide intervention, we hold pre-consulting interviews. During these interviews, we try our best to uncover some of the issues and problems faced by the employees in the company.

It is sometimes quite challenging as many people are reluctant to reveal details. When asked the problems they currently face, more often than not, they will put on a smile and say that the environment is wonderful. Everyone has worked together for so long, they are almost like a family! No problems at all. To probe them a little more, we typically ask what were some of their biggest complaints during tea breaks and lunch times. Then the revelations begin to pour forth.

Typical problems like the little story above will be revealed. The lack of trust is one of the strongest hindrance to success. Conversely, strong trust can bring about the most positive of teams.

While customizing a team development program for a company, I learnt that the reason for the program was a lack of trust in a new manager. This new manager was the source of numerous resignations. What I proposed was to design the program with a great deal of focus on leaders and followers. That would help build the trust needed in bridging the gap. After the program ended, the team was united. They finally understood that this manager was trying to implement some changes and they also understood why he was doing it. Sometimes, the time spent in taking a break somewhere just to unwind and share with one another will be able to build trust.

During another team session, a new team leader, in a bid to build up the trust of his team, stood up towards the end of the session to address his new team members. He told them that he wanted to win their trust. I remember clearly his line. "The first mistake that you make, will be my mistake." That one line broke the tension between the team members and the new leader. They realized that he was someone they could rely on and go to for discussion.

Besides in the boardroom or during work, trust can and must be built outside the working environment. During an overnight training session, the leader of a new team decided to let her hair down. During the night session, she paid for everyone to go dancing and singing. Despite her not being able to dance or sing in tune, she knew that that was not the point, it was what the team wanted to do that was important. She learnt to dance during that session!

In order to build trust, everyone needs to take the effort to go out of their comfort zone and find out more about one another. Coupled with the eagerness to help others and ask others for help, trust can be built. Once built, teams can soar.

The only way to make a man trustworthy is to trust him. - Henry Stimson

TAKEAWAYS

- Encourage trust and cooperation among members on your team. Remember that the relationships team members establish among themselves are every bit as important as those you establish with them. As the team begins to take shape, pay close attention to the ways in which different team members work together and take steps to improve communication, cooperation, trust and respect in those relationships
- Facilitate communication. Remember that communication is the single most important factor in building trust. Facilitating communication does not mean holding meetings all the time. Instead it means setting an example by remaining open to suggestions and concerns, by asking questions and offering help, and by doing everything you can to avoid confusion in your own communication

Chapter Four: Great Teams have Open Communication

The Story

A new General Manager, Mr Holdur Tonguee, has just taken over Openness Ltd.

As he began his opening address to the 80 employees of Openness Ltd, he opened his hands wide open and told everyone that he believed in an open door policy. As valued employees, they could speak openly to him anytime.

He also planned to schedule round table dialogues when they could voice out their concerns and difficulties.

The employees applauded in excitement as they could sense a positive change in the air.

From the following day onwards, the employees noticed that the GM's door was indeed always open. When the first bold employee tried to share his new idea with the GM, Mr Holdur Tongue dismissed the idea as something that would never work. Soon, an invisible door was covering the open door.

When the first round table discussion came, some employees questioned some policies within the organization. The following week saw these employees clearing their desks. Soon, the round table dialogue became a monologue.

The lack of open communication began set in between management and staff. Like a disease, it soon spread among department heads and followed by staff within the departments. Everyone only believed in their own Key Performance Indicators. It became a "me, myself and I" policy. Everyone became strangers.

It was an irony that the slogan of Openness Ltd was "We Open your Door to Communication".

MEDIOCRITY VERSUS GREATNESS
Great Teams have Open Communication

Open Communication is nothing new. In fact, many organizations believe that they uphold open communication. How do they do that? They sometimes begin by starting with a CEO dialogue session, a monthly gathering where CEO is supposed to share the vision of the company. They may verbally mention an open-door policy. But it usually stops there.

By the next working day, bosses are walking around the office, taking note of employees not seated at their tables or glued to their computer screen and watching for those who leave the office to go home on time.

In a culture like that, open communication is not present. When open communication is not present, people will become task focused. The plus point is that certain things may get accomplished, but the zeal behind the tasks, the willingness to stretch beyond one's capabilities will not be there. Everyone bottles up their thoughts, concerns and most drastically, good ideas.

This creates what I call the "Silo Syndrome". Every department works as a silo. It becomes a "me, myself and I" culture. Where the enemy is no longer the business environment, or the competitor, but it becomes the department next door.

I remember someone from such an organization mentioning to me that they did not need competitors to tear them apart. They can achieve it happily on their own!

What a frightening thought!

Open communication encourages teams and individuals to share and learn. Instead of seeing their part as just what they must do, they begin to see what more they can do for the team.

For open communication to begin, it should certainly be a top-down approach. Someone high enough up the ladder must start the ball rolling. First, he or she must believe that it is necessary. Then the ball can begin to roll.

I remember a training session I conducted with a group of management staff from an MNC. The new MD had just taken over from someone else. During the session, many of the staff were wary of saying too much for fear of this new and relatively serious leader. After the first day, we ran an activity on leaders and followers. The main debrief point for the activity was the need to build open communication.

When everyone understood the importance of open communication, I invited him forward to address the group. He then proceeded to mention that as he was new, he was also learning. He wanted to learn from the entire team. He also said that he welcomed open communication. He wanted more ideas and suggestions from everyone. He promised to take their ideas and feedback seriously. The moment he ended, everyone applauded. What a change it was from the earlier day! More importantly, what a change that would make to the future of the company!

Another experience I had was training a cross-cultural team of engineers. They comprised people from countries from Asia, Middle East, Europe and America. When it came to an experiential activity, it was almost impossible for the team to achieve the task. The differences between the members were obvious. Some were not so open and tended to keep their ideas within themselves and sometimes they even discussed within their small groups in their own native languages. Others were more open in sharing of the ideas, but they also discussed among themselves. They could do little to get the others to execute what was being planned. After a short while, I paused the activity. Even though the group agreed to have open communication based on what they learnt earlier, it was still not happening. We agreed that discussion should be done in a common language, which in that case, was English. Ideas should be shared openly, and a leader should rise among the group to lead the discussion and planning. They all agreed to make those changes.

The activity restarted. This time, a young man stood on a platform to take the "lead". He asked for ideas and suggestions. Everyone listened to the different options being presented, and then they decided through consensus to execute the best plan. Once that was done, they allocated themselves into several working groups and executed the task with one person coordinating everything.

Open communication is truly possible. But it will take some effort. That effort must come from everyone.

The single biggest problem in communication is the illusion that it has taken place. - George Bernard Shaw

TAKEAWAYS

- Team members must listen and pay attention to one another. There should never be people on the "sidelines"
- Ideas and suggestions are collective, not individualistic
- It is impossible that the best ideas is going to come from the top management
- People who share to improve their working environment actually benefit themselves in the long run
- Everyone should be given a chance to state his or her views
- Members should be clear about group decisions. When in doubt, ask questions
- Everyone must be committed to the decision made by the Team
- Frequent feedback should be given to help members stay focused on team goals
- Appointed leaders need not be the "expert" in the topic at hand
- Try not to argue or criticize. Instead build on other people's ideas – that will build open communication

Chapter Five: Great Teams Think Positive

The Story

A small team of managers from Motivation Center Ltd were looking into the issue of solving some process breakdowns.

They gathered together for a meeting. Mr Gary Gloom started off the session by asking everyone to share what they felt about the problem. With a grim look on their faces, each of them shared about the difficulties they faced, the problems along the way and all the possible scenarios of the process breaking down.

Ms Bright then suggested some ways of re-looking at the same problem. They could isolate the different issues and form a few task groups to tackle each of them. She shared with the team several other companies' experiences in solving similar problems.

The team looked at her disbelievingly. Was she hard of hearing? Mr Gary Gloom then told her that they were not "like" other companies. What they faced was unique. It was uniquely their own problem and a straightforward solution was not so easily available!

It was a rather doom and gloom meeting as everyone agreed wholeheartedly with one another that the task was not only difficult to solve, but literally impossible!

Two months after the meeting, the problem remained, everyone suffered, business suffered and Ms Bright left the company after realizing that her future elsewhere was brighter.

MEDIOCRITY VERSUS GREATNESS

Great Teams Think Positive

Positivity is a rare commodity in today's fast-paced world. Everyday we're bombarded with negative thoughts and negative news. How often have we watched the evening news and the newscaster actually mentioned positive news throughout the session? Almost never. In today's context, people seem to thrive on negative news.

Negativity will prevent our team success. It takes only one person to frown or to give up and somehow, that one person can influence the rest of the team. One yawn is enough to pull down the morale of an entire team. Negativity is contagious.

I remember a team challenge where everyone was tied up tightly together and had to move around as a group to collect treasures. Halfway through, when everyone looked tired and demoralized, a sixty-year-old gentleman in the team encouraged everyone not to give up. It was an amazing scene: a person twice the age of more than half the team began raising the spirit of a team that felt it was going to be defeated.

Sometimes in my work, I get the chance to facilitate the department issues and communication problems of teams. On one such occasion, the company had two departments that were at loggerheads with each other. There was tension and a breakdown in communication. In fact, many of them communicated only via emails and even refused to speak to one another.

When we began the ice-breakers, the atmosphere was cordial. There came a time when I decided that it was necessary to have an activity to draw out their appreciation for each other. They were tasked to write positive things about each other on little notes and pass to each other. This began the healing process. At the end of the two days, the two warring factions began to see each other positively. They began to converge, and became the One team that they were meant to be! It started when everyone began to view each other in a positive light!

Sometimes, positivity comes easily for some people, but tougher for others. To build a positive attitude, sometimes it just takes some reflection to see where we belong.

I had a training session where the focus was on building passion in a team. During a segment when participants took time to reflect on their level of passion for their work, one participant approached me and told me that he had zero passion for his work. He found no goal and objective in the team he was in.

I began to share with him that sometimes we may not be able to choose where we work, but we can certainly choose how we work. From there, I told him that the people around him would be what matters most at the end of every day. I gave him a scenario: Supposing one day we leave the team, what would we like to see happen? Would we like people in the company to be sad that you have to leave, but yet wish you all the best for your future, or would you like the people in the company hold a celebration when you leave?!

He started to see things differently after that morning's sharing. By the end of the two-day program, I could see a change in him. Acquaintances around him became friends. The entire process started when he began to see things positively.

When everyone in a team begins to think positive, a great team emerges!

Enthusiasm is excitement with inspiration, motivation, and a pinch of creativity. - Bo Bennett

TAKEAWAYS

- Encourage team members to look at situations from different angles
- We choose and wear our clothes every morning. Attitude is the same. Positivity is an attitude – we can choose to wear it every morning
- Leaders must lead by example. Leaders must be positive and then the team will head in the right direction
- Believe in positive feedback as it is the only constructive feedback
- Put on a smile, it takes a lot less muscles to smile then to frown!

The Final Diagnosis

T his is a common story, but certainly worth repeating. Many years ago, I had the opportunity to see a flock of geese flying in the sky. They flew in the famous flying "V" formation. What is amazing about the formation is that there is a great deal of teamwork involved.

HERE ARE JUST SOME of the interesting facts.

Firstly, as each bird flaps its wings, it creates uplift for the next bird following behind. By flying in a "V" formation, the entire flock actually increases the range for flying by over 70 percent than if one bird had flown alone.

What is the lesson we can learn from this? People need to share a common direction. In that way, the destination can be reached quicker and easier because they are traveling on the strength of one another.

Secondly, whenever a goose falls out of formation, it will feel the drag and resistance of flying alone. Hence, it will want to get back into formation as quickly as possible. This is so that it can take full advantage of the lifting power of the birds flying in front.

This is equivalent to people who are willing to accept the help of others as well as give help to others when in need.

Third, when the lead goose gets tired, it will fly to the back of the "V" formation and automatically, another goose will take its position in the front of the formation.

What this teaches us is that we need to take turns at doing different tasks and that leadership is not a one-person-burden, but a shared one.

Everyone has their part to play, and this may include trusting the head and passing the vision down the line.

Finally, the geese in formation honk from behind to encourage those up front to keep on going. In teams, we need to make sure our honking can be heard. Not only that, it should be encouraging and positive. No negativity or complaining!

Let's ask ourselves this: if we were geese flying in the air, would we be in "V" formation? Or perhaps "W" or "X"!

Let's put action to transform our teams today! From Team Mediocrity to Team Greatness!

If geese can do it, so can we!

The End

About the Author

Marako Marcus loves using anecdotal stories, pragmatic tips, straight talk style of writing! He endeavours to put out bite-sized handbooks to help people around the world. Each handbook should be placed somewhere on the bookshelf, so that it can be used as a just-in-time reference.

Marako has over 25-year experience as a management consultant and career coach. He works with organizations around the world, developing people-centric interventions, improving the way of working, enabling creative synergies through diversity. He is also author of books and articles on creativity and teamwork, and an engaging speaker at conferences.

He is also an avid musician and composer, creating stories and experiences onto a musical canvas. He writes instrumental music for listeners to feel relaxed, rested and inspired. All his music are available on all major streaming platforms.

Connect with Marako Marcus

I really appreciate you reading my book!

YOU CAN FIND ME AT:
LinkedIn: https://www.linkedin.com/in/marakomarcus
Twitter: https://twitter.com/marakomarcus
Instagram: https://instagram.com/marakomarcus
Website: https://www.marakomarcus.com

Printed in Great Britain
by Amazon